DATE DUE

PRINTED IN U.S.A.

D1364737

The NFL's Greatest Teams

NEW YORK GIANTS

Marcia Zappa

Big Buddy Books
An Imprint of Abdo Publishing
www.abdopublishing.com

www.abdopublishing.com

Published by Abdo Publishing, a division of ABDO, PO Box 398166, Minneapolis, Minnesota 55439.
Copyright © 2015 by Abdo Consulting Group, Inc. International copyrights reserved in all countries. No part
of this book may be reproduced in any form without written permission from the publisher. Big Buddy Books™
is a trademark and logo of Abdo Publishing.

Printed in the United States of America, North Mankato, Minnesota.
042014
092014

THIS BOOK CONTAINS
RECYCLED MATERIALS

Cover Photo: ASSOCIATED PRESS.
Interior Photos: ASSOCIATED PRESS.

Coordinating Series Editor: Rochelle Baltzer
Contributing Editors: Bridget O'Brien, Sarah Tieck
Graphic Design: Michelle Labatt

Library of Congress Cataloging-in-Publication Data

Zappa, Marcia, 1985-
  New York Giants / Marcia Zappa.
    pages cm. -- (The NFL's greatest teams)
  ISBN 978-1-62403-364-3
1. New York Giants (Football team)--History--Juvenile literature. I. Title.
  GV956.N4Z37 2015
  796.332'64097471--dc23
                      2013051242

Contents

A Winning Team

The New York Giants are a football team from New York City, New York. They have played in the National Football League (NFL) for more than 85 years.

The Giants have had good seasons and bad. But time and again, they've proven themselves. Let's see what makes the Giants one of the NFL's greatest teams.

Blue, red, white, and gray are the team's colors.

Home Field Advantage

The Giants play home games in New Jersey. It is near New York City. But, it has more space for a large stadium.

League Play

Team Standings

The NFC and the American Football Conference (AFC) make up the NFL. Each conference has a north, south, east, and west division.

The NFL got its start in 1920. Its teams have changed over the years. Today, there are 32 teams. These teams make up two conferences and eight divisions.

The Giants play in the East Division of the National Football Conference (NFC). This division also includes the Dallas Cowboys, the Philadelphia Eagles, and the Washington Redskins.

The Eagles have long been a rival of the Giants.

Fans get excited to watch their team play!

Kicking Off

The Giants started out in 1925. The team was founded by Tim Mara. They played at the Polo Grounds in New York City. The Giants quickly became a strong team.

Early on, the Giants were important to the NFL's success. By being in the country's largest city, they brought a lot of fans to the league.

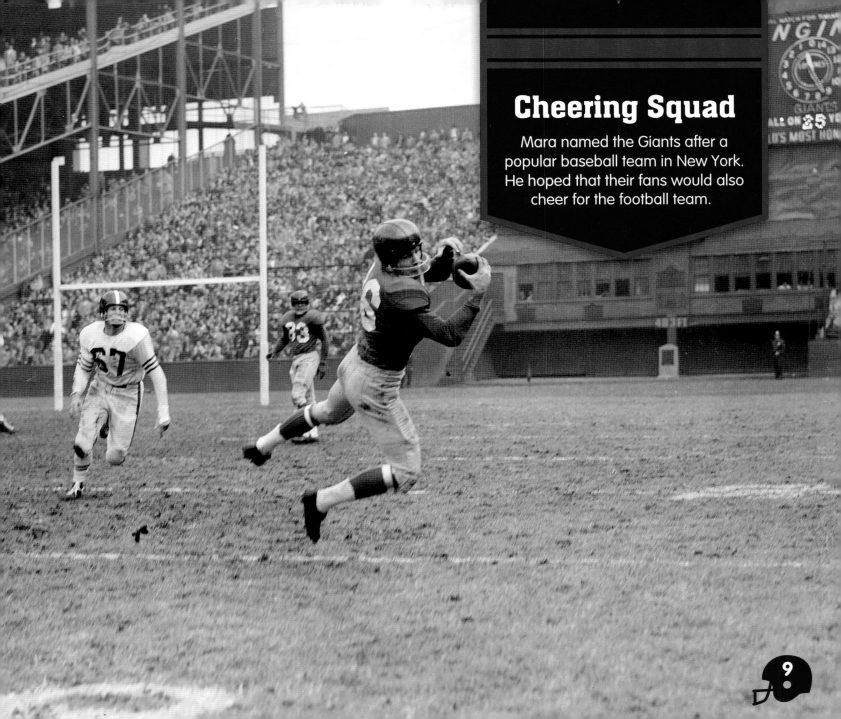

Cheering Squad

Mara named the Giants after a popular baseball team in New York. He hoped that their fans would also cheer for the football team.

Highlight Reel

In 1927, the Giants won the NFL **championship**. Their powerful defense allowed only 20 points in 13 games that season!

The Giants were champions again in 1934 and 1938. But, they didn't win another championship until 1956.

The team's success ended after 1963. From 1964 to 1980, the Giants had only two winning seasons.

Win or Go Home

NFL teams play 16 regular season games each year. The teams with the best records are part of the play-off games. Play-off winners move on to the conference championship. Then, conference winners face off in the Super Bowl!

In 1958, the Giants lost the championship game to the Baltimore Colts by six points. Many people consider this close game to be one of the NFL's best.

The 1934 championship game is called the "Sneakers Game." The Giants wore basketball shoes to keep from slipping on the icy ground.

11

The Giants won their first Super Bowl in 1987. They beat the Denver Broncos 39–20. The team returned to the Super Bowl in 1991. They beat the Buffalo Bills 20–19.

The Giants didn't do very well for the rest of the 1990s. In 2001, they returned to the Super Bowl. But, they lost 34–7 to the Baltimore Ravens.

In 2004, coach Tom Coughlin and quarterback Eli Manning joined the Giants. They led the team back to the Super Bowl in 2008. The Giants beat the **undefeated** New England Patriots 17–14!

The Giants beat the Patriots again in the 2012 Super Bowl. They won 21–17.

Halftime! Stat Break

Team Records

RUSHING YARDS
Career: Tiki Barber, 10,449 yards (1997–2006)
Single Season: Tiki Barber, 1,860 yards (2005)
PASSING YARDS
Career: Eli Manning, 35,345 yards and gaining (2004–)
Single Season: Eli Manning, 4,933 yards (2011)
RECEPTIONS
Career: Amani Toomer, 668 receptions (1996–2008)
Single Season: Steve Smith, 107 receptions (2009)
ALL-TIME LEADING SCORER
Pete Gogolak, 646 points (1966–1974)

Famous Coaches

Steve Owen (1930–1953)
Bill Parcells (1983–1990)
Tom Coughlin (2004–)

Championships

EARLY CHAMPIONSHIP WINS:
1927, 1934, 1938, 1956

SUPER BOWL APPEARANCES:
1987, 1991, 2001, 2008, 2012

SUPER BOWL WINS:
1987, 1991, 2008, 2012

Pro Football Hall of Famers & Their Years with the Giants

Morris "Red" Badgro, End (1930–1935)
Roosevelt Brown, Offensive Tackle (1953–1965)
Harry Carson, Linebacker (1976–1988)
Benny Friedman, Quarterback (1929–1931)
Frank Gifford, Halfback (1952–1960, 1962–1964)
Mel Hein, Center (1931–1945)
Sam Huff, Linebacker (1956–1963)
Alphonse "Tuffy" Leemans, Halfback-Fullback (1936–1943)
Wellington Mara, Owner/Administrator (1937–2005)
Tim Mara, Founder/Owner (1925–1959)
Steve Owen, Tackle (1926–1931, 1933), Coach (1930–1953)
Bill Parcells, Coach (1983–1990)
Andy Robustelli, Defensive End (1956–1964)
Ken Strong, Halfback (1933–1935, 1939, 1944–1947)
Fran Tarkenton, Quarterback (1967–1971)
Lawrence Taylor, Linebacker (1981–1993)
Y.A. Tittle, Quarterback (1961–1964)
Emlen Tunnell, Safety (1948–1958)
Arnie Weinmeister, Defensive Tackle (1950–1953)

Fan Fun

NICKNAMES: G-Men, Big Blue
STADIUM: MetLife Stadium
LOCATION: East Rutherford, New Jersey

Coaches' Corner

Steve Owen was first a star player for the Giants. In 1930, he became the head coach. Owen coached the team for 23 years. He led the Giants to many winning seasons. This included two NFL **championships**.

Bill Parcells became head coach for the Giants in 1983. After one losing season, he turned the team around. He led them to their first Super Bowl win in 1987. After the Giants won a second Super Bowl in 1991, Parcells left the team.

After a big win in 1987, players dumped Gatorade on coach Parcells. This practice started after a Giants game in 1985.

Tom Coughlin began coaching the Giants in 2004.

Star Players

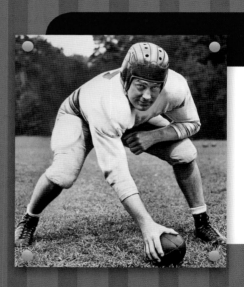

Mel Hein   CENTER (1931–1945)

Mel Hein didn't miss a single game in his 15 seasons with the Giants. He won the NFL's Most Valuable Player (MVP) award in 1938. Hein is the only offensive lineman to win this award. In 1963, he became one of the first members of the Pro Football Hall of Fame.

Emlen Tunnell SAFETY (1948–1958)

Emlen Tunnell played for the Giants for 11 seasons. He was known for his many **interceptions**. In 1967, Tunnell became the first African-American member of the Pro Football Hall of Fame.

Lawrence Taylor LINEBACKER (1981–1993)

Lawrence Taylor was the team's first pick in the 1981 **draft**. He helped the Giants win their first two Super Bowls. Taylor was named the NFL's MVP in 1986. And, he was named the NFL's Defensive Player of the Year three times.

Phil Simms QUARTERBACK (1979–1993)

As starting quarterback, Phil Simms led the Giants to their first Super Bowl! In the game, he completed 22 out of 25 passes. He was named the game's MVP.

Michael Strahan DEFENSIVE END (1993–2007)

Michael Strahan played for the Giants his whole **career**. In 2001, he got 22.5 sacks. That is the NFL single-season record! He was named the NFL's Defensive Player of the Year. He helped his team reach the Super Bowl twice and win once.

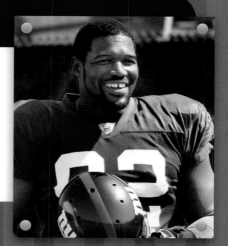

Tiki Barber RUNNING BACK (1997–2006)

Tiki Barber played for the Giants for ten seasons. During that time, he rushed for 10,449 yards. That is more than any other Giant. Barber was also a skilled receiver and punt returner. He helped the team reach the Super Bowl in 2001.

Eli Manning QUARTERBACK (2004–)

Eli Manning became the team's starting quarterback in 2004. He has more passing yards and touchdown passes than any other Giant. Manning led the team to two Super Bowl wins. He was named MVP in both games.

MetLife Stadium

The New York Giants play home games at MetLife Stadium. It is in East Rutherford, New Jersey. MetLife Stadium opened in 2010. It can hold about 82,500 people. The New York Jets also play home games there.

MetLife Stadium hosted the Super Bowl in 2014.

METLIFE STADIUM

23

Go Big Blue!

Thousands of fans go to MetLife Stadium to see the Giants play home games. Some fans call their team "the G-Men" or "Big Blue." Sometimes, fireworks explode around the stadium.

MetLife Stadium can be very cold and snowy in the winter. So, fans have to bundle up to stay warm.

Fan Food

Fans enjoy local favorite foods at home games. This includes pork rolls, meatballs, and pepper and egg sandwiches.

Final Call

The New York Giants have a long, rich history. They were NFL **champions** many times during their early years. The team became champions again in the 1980s and the 2000s.

Even during losing seasons, true fans have stuck with them. Many believe that the New York Giants will remain one of the NFL's greatest teams.

SUPER BOWL XLVI
CHAMPIONS

Giants fans are proud of their team's four Super Bowl wins.

Through the Years

1927
The team wins its first NFL **championship**.

1956
The team begins playing home games at Yankee Stadium. Before this, the Polo Grounds had been their home field.

1963
Tim Mara and Mel Hein become original members of the Pro Football Hall of Fame.

1925
Tim Mara founds the New York Giants.

1936
The Giants take part in the NFL's first **draft**. Their first pick is tackle Art Lewis.

2012

The Giants win their fourth Super Bowl.

2008

The Giants surprise fans by beating the New England Patriots in the Super Bowl.

1976

Giants Stadium in East Rutherford, New Jersey, becomes the Giants home field.

1990

Lawrence Taylor is chosen to play in the Pro Bowl for the tenth time. That is more than any other Giant.

1987

The Giants win their first Super Bowl.

29

Postgame Recap

1. Who was the coach of the Giants when they won their first Super Bowl?
   A. Bill Parcells   **B**. Steve Owen   **C**. Tom Coughlin

2. What is the name of the stadium where the New York Giants play their home games?
   A. Giants Stadium   **B**. MetLife Stadium   **C**. New Meadowlands Stadium

3. Where is it located?
   A. New York City, New York
   B. Rochester, New York
   C. East Rutherford, New Jersey

4. Name 3 of the 19 Giants in the Pro Football Hall of Fame.

5. Why were the Giants important to the success of the NFL in the early years?
   A. Being in a big city, they attracted lots of star players.
   B. They were the first team on the East Coast.
   C. Being in a big city, they attracted lots of new fans.

1. A 2. B 3. C 4. See page 15 5. C.

Glossary

career work a person does to earn money for living.

champion the winner of a championship, which is a game, a match, or a race held to find a first-place winner.

draft a system for professional sports teams to choose new players. When a team drafts a player, they choose that player for their team.

interception (ihn-tuhr-SEHP-shuhn) when a player catches a pass that was meant for the other team's player.

undefeated not having any losses.

Websites

To learn more about the NFL's Greatest Teams, visit **booklinks.abdopublishing.com**. These links are routinely monitored and updated to provide the most current information available.

Index